APPLE TIME

and other
Hidden Pictures
puzzles

HIGHLIGHTS PRESS
AN IMPRINT OF HIGHLIGHTS
Honesdale, Pennsylvania

Welcome, Hidden Pictures® puzzlers!

You've come to the right place. Inside, you'll find dozens of classic Hidden Pictures puzzles with more than 450 hidden objects to find.

When you finish a puzzle, check it off √. Good luck, and happy puzzling!

Contents

Cover: "Apple Time" by Mike Moran

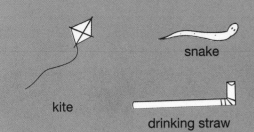
kite

snake

necktie

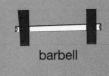
barbell

mug

camera

knitted hat

seashell

pencil

Turning Out Turnovers

sock

cane

zipper

olive

umbrella

pennant

yo-yo

3

toothbrush

banana

shoe

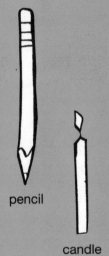
pencil

candle

open book

Snow Day

paper clip

caterpillar

bell

kite

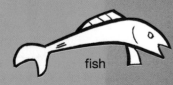
fish

glove

slice of pie

heart

slice of bread

comb

ice-cream cone

needle

light bulb

cowboy hat

saw

eyeglasses

frog

snake

Illustrated by Tim Davis

5

Bunny B-Ball

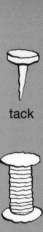

tack

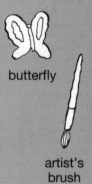

spool of thread

butterfly

artist's brush

spoon

feather

button

carrot

slice of pie

banana

glove

spatula

bell

flying disk

ring

flashlight

6

Illustrated by David Helton

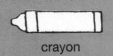
crayon

pitcher

ruler

car

swim goggles

wishbone

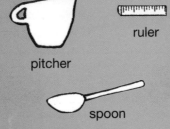
spoon

pail

light bulb

bell

Bubble Buddies

Illustrated by John Nez

shovel

nail

paper clip

lock

croquet mallet

horseshoe

broccoli

paper airplane

7

Slow Climb

bell

oar

banana

sock

crescent moon

needle

golf club

fishhook

frying pan

pennant

candle

shoe

fish

spoon

slice of bread

Illustrated by Mike DeSantis

sailboat

book

fish

snow cone

butterfly

magnet

flag

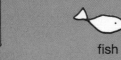
banana

saw

envelope

saltshaker

crown

New Clothes

mug

drinking straw

hammer

crescent moon

carrot

Illustrated by Marilee Harrald-Pilz

9

Pumpkin Portraits

nail

fork

chick

lemon

pencil

key

comb

swim fin

bat

book

magnet

banana

teddy bear

hot dog

fried egg

ruler

10

Illustrated by Marc Nadel

frying pan

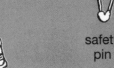
spool of thread

safety pin

carrot

telescope

book

Hockey on the Pond

pushpin

shovel

funnel

ice-cream cone

candle

slice of cake

Illustrated by Charles Jordan

mug

flashlight

glove

pencil

crown

envelope

wedge of lemon

At the Dog Park

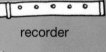
recorder

wishbone

12

bottle

heart

slice of
pizza

carrot

fork

toothbrush

banana

baseball bat

seashell

open book

paper clip

spoon

golf club

whale

cupcake

artist's brush

fish

snail

funnel

candle

crescent moon

key

Illustrated by Maggie Swanson

Nutty for Peanuts

hockey stick

hot dog

crown

lightning bolt

mushroom

comb

boomerang

nail

olive

book

ring

ice-cream bar

handbell

trowel

question mark

artist's brush

sailboat

arrow

14

Illustrated by Marilyn Janovitz

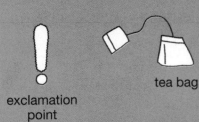
exclamation
point

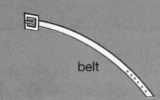
tea bag

belt

candy kiss

mug

four-leaf
clover

magnet

button

arrowhead

apple core

leaf

bird

Eye to Eye

Illustrated by Paul Richer

Wrong Turn

crescent moon

handbell

feather

light bulb

pennant

sailboat

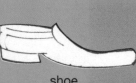
shoe

spoon

shuttlecock

safety pin

heart

bowl

tooth

baseball cap

banana

egg

16

birdhouse

slice of pizza

pair of shorts

sheep

toothbrush

comb

golf club

To the Rescue

sailboat

sock

pencil

ice-cream
cone

wedge of
lemon

nail

musical
note

Illustrated by R. Michael Palan

17

boot

book

drinking glass

ring

screw

peppermint
stick

pear

flag

paper clip

iron

cherry

bowl

light bulb

stick of candy

muffin

domino

banana

spool of thread

wedge of lemon

Illustrated by Arieh Zeldich

button

coffeepot

heart

egg

crescent moon

19

Backstage Show

badge

wristwatch

spatula

bell

banana

pennant

bowl

ring

domino

feather

snake

envelope

sock

paintbrush

flashlight

needle

sailboat

pencil

ruler

20

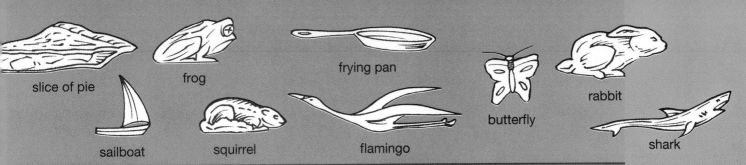

slice of pie

frog

frying pan

sailboat

squirrel

flamingo

butterfly

rabbit

shark

Iguana Steps Out

palm tree

hat

slice of watermelon

pointy hat

eagle's head

angelfish

football

Illustrated by Joe Seidita

Time for School

flag

heart

toothbrush

spatula

lollipop

open book

bear's head

pennant

trowel

pencil

wishbone

sailboat

ladder

sheep

drinking straw

cupcake

slice of cake

22

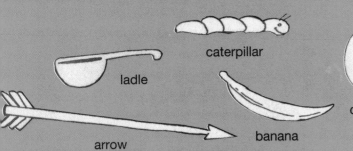
ladle

caterpillar

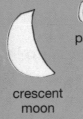
crescent moon

paper clip

tack

mushroom

arrow

banana

button

carrot

envelope

ring

fishhook

Balloons for Sale

lollipop

cane

flag

toothbrush

needle

nail

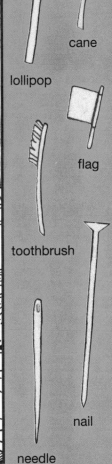

Illustrated by Maxim Mitrofanov

magnifying glass

squirrel

safety pin

pear

toothbrush

rabbit

Animal Circus

CD

fish

2 combs

bow

snake

bowl

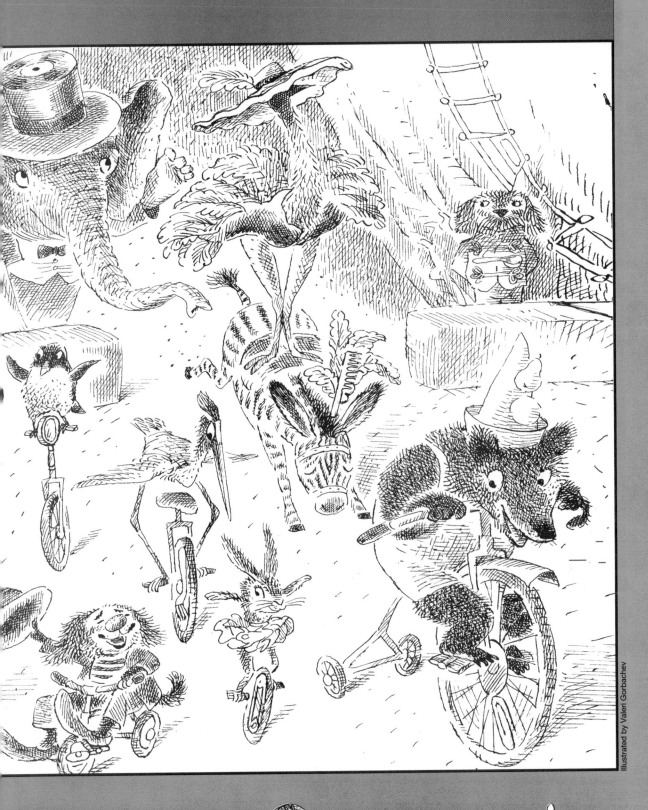

Illustrated by Valeri Gorbachev

sailboat

nail

artist's brush

iron

bell

mouse

3 frogs

seal

paper clip

fork

spoon

25

On the Midway

cane

toothbrush

teacup

heart

closed umbrella

needle

snake

mushroom

nail

canoe

book

pencil

ring

crescent moon

arrow

26

Illustrated by Sally Springer

shoe

pear

bell

cotton candy

wristwatch

ring

mitten

pennant

dart

wishbone

crescent moon

envelope

slice of pizza

four-leaf clover

eyeglasses

sock

teacup

slice of cake

wrench

arrow

needle

olive

pencil

artist's brush

peppermint stick

ax

candle

carrot

heart

bowl

S'mores for All!

Illustrated by Diana Zourelias

27

Get on Board

Illustrated by Stacy Curtis

heart

carrot

bowling ball

golf club

broccoli

envelope

wishbone

colander

magnet

lollipop

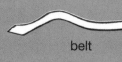
crown

belt

domino

button

slice of watermelon

glove

spool of thread

football

doughnut

cookie

eyeglasses

high-heeled
shoe

mug

cupcake

banana

loaf of bread

kite

tent

saucepan

beret

Long Weekend

chicken

hot dog

harp

coin purse

hat

saw

comb

rolling pin

Illustrated by Kathy Swain-O'Brien

29

teapot

briefcase

seashell

crown

spoon

teacup

clothespin

And the Winner Is . . .

saw

baseball

feather

button

walnut

mushroom

bell

rolling pin

ice-cream
cone

wishbone

saltshaker

butterfly

doughnut

coat hanger

Illustrated by Marc Nadel

pen

candle

slice of bread

star

light bulb

broccoli

snake

31

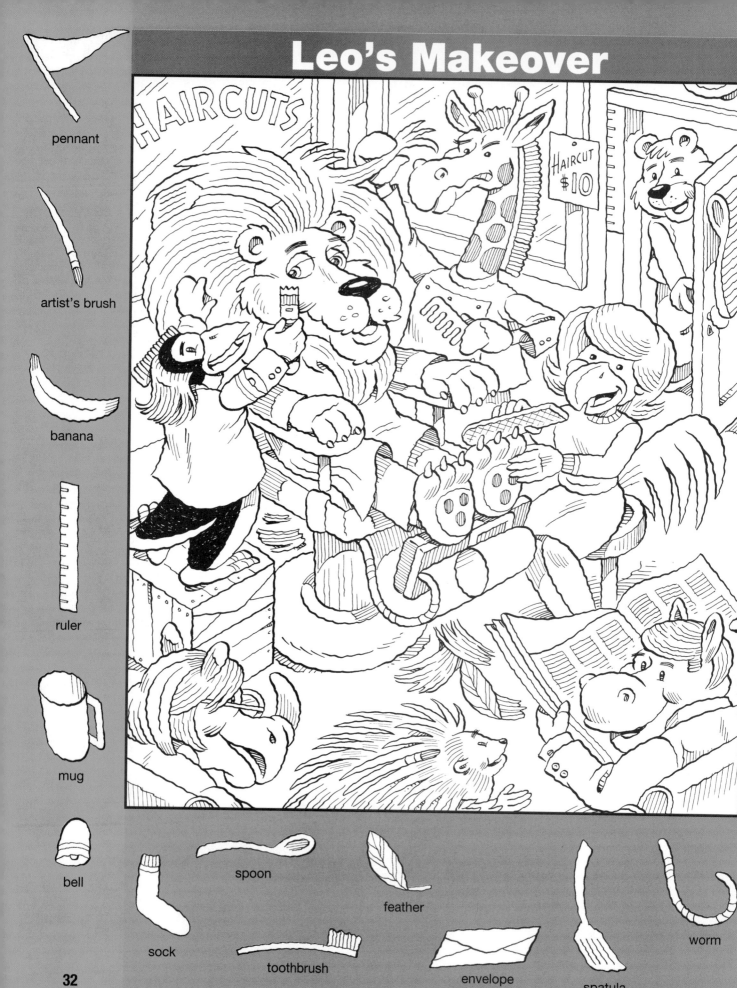

pennant

artist's brush

banana

ruler

mug

bell

sock

spoon

feather

toothbrush

envelope

spatula

worm

Illustrated by David Helton

Dragon Parade

ghost

candle

owl

crescent moon

worm

pretzel

baseball

bird

fish

mitten

snow cone

pencil

star

frog

carrot

artist's palette

elephant

Illustrated by Susan T. Hall

Orang Umbrellas

carrot

mushroom

ice-cream bar

fishhook

baseball cap

paintbrush

octopus

bowl

vase

bird

bell

pennant

fish

ax

34

Illustrated by Katy Piemmons

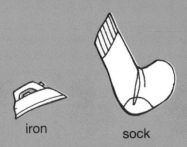
iron

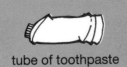
sock

tube of toothpaste

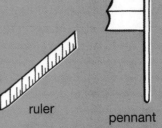
eyeglasses

ruler

pennant

toothbrush

harmonica

bottle of lotion

flashlight

ring

heart

snow cone

artist's brush

crown

Room to Create

Illustrated by Susan Dahlman

35

Balancing Act

heart

paintbrush

ice-cream cone

horn

candle

crescent moon

egg

banana

pencil

doughnut

fish

kite

spoon

flag

dog

Illustrated by Tim Davis

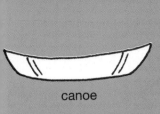
canoe

frying pan

ring

caterpillar

spoon

magnet

feather

fish

waffle

book

toothbrush

duck

needle

paintbrush

acorn

Hat Shop

Illustrated by Mike DeSantis

37

Look! Lemurs!

crown

comb

sheep

muffin

ice-cream
cone

rabbit

closed umbrella

pennant

mug

belt

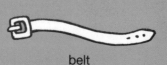

2 fish

screwdriver

artist's brush

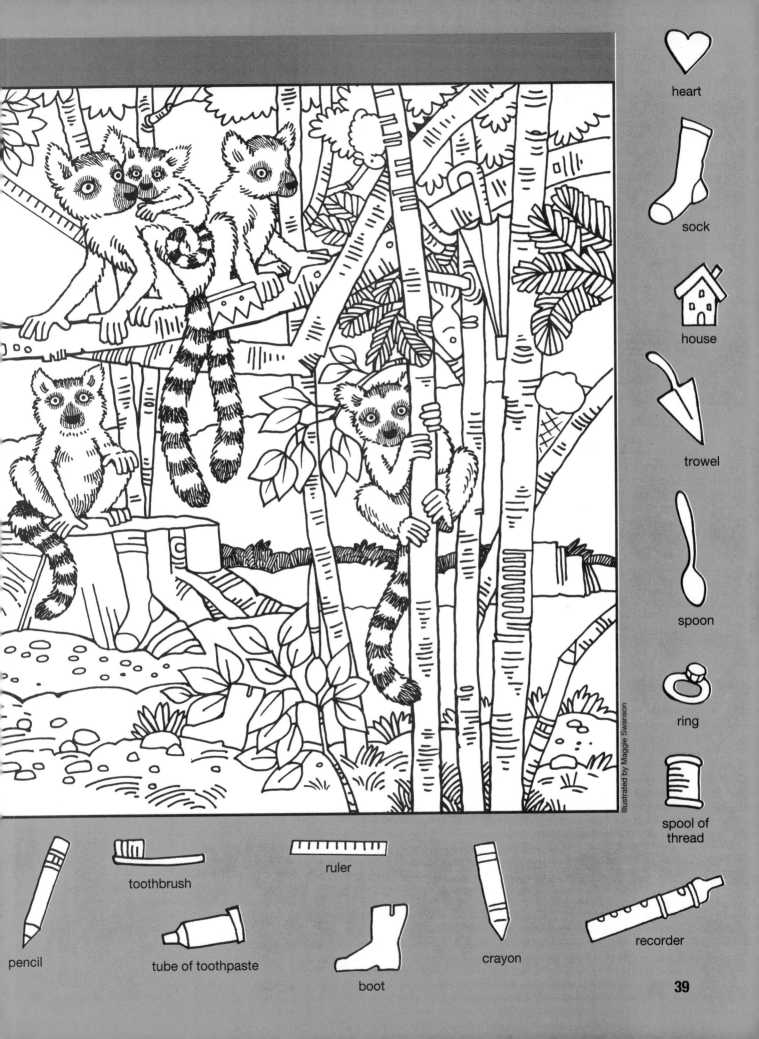

heart

sock

house

trowel

spoon

ring

spool of thread

toothbrush

ruler

pencil

tube of toothpaste

boot

crayon

recorder

Illustrated by Maggie Swanson

Pottery Class

tube of toothpaste

boot

cupcake

hockey stick

sailboat

mitten

comb

fishhook

mushroom

musical note

40

screwdriver

toothbrush

pencil

toy top

slice of pie

bumblebee

jar

tack

hat

crown

artist's brush

pennant

whale

candle

handbe

Illustrated by Linda Weller

ladle
ruler

paper clip

eyeglasses

banana

feather

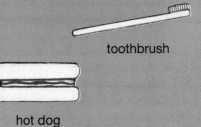
hot dog

toothbrush

carrot

Pass the Wasabi

monkey's head

butterfly

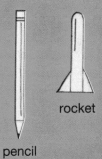
pencil

rocket

fried egg

snow cone

sock

crown

Illustrated by Barbara Samuels

Autumn Treats

ring

ruler

saw

inchworm

suitcase

comb

glove

spatula

sailboat

wedge of
watermelon

flag

lollipop

domino

bowl

carrot

saltshaker

magnet

42

Answers

▼ Page 3

▼ Pages 4–5

▼ Page 6

▼ Page 7

▼ Page 8

▼ Page 9

▼ Page 10

▼ Page 11

Answers

▼Pages 12–13

▼Page 14

▼Page 15

▼Page 16

▼Page 17

▼Pages 18–19

▼Page 20

▼Page 21

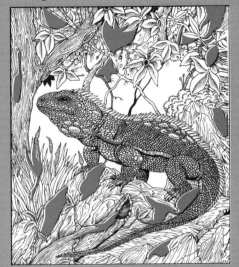

▼Page 22

▼Page 23

▼Pages 24–25

▼Page 26

Answers

▼Page 27

▼Page 28

▼Page 29

▼Pages 30–31

▼Page 32

▼Page 33

▼Page 34

▼Page 35

▼Page 36

▼Page 37

▼Pages 38–39

▼Page 40

Answers

▼Page 41

▼Page 42

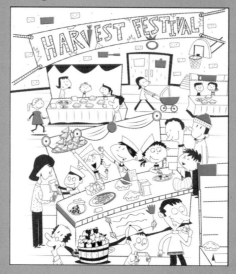